The Gift of Enough

A Journal for the Present Moment

Terry Hershey

franciscan
media
Cincinnati, Ohio

To Live Simply. To Simply Live.

I love to write. Since I was a boy, paper and pencil have been on my list of favorite things. Now, I've added a nib pen. As a boy, I journaled. I still do. Some years, writing every day.

All journals have this in common: They give voice to what is inside. They become safe space. In that way, journaling is like a sanctuary: a time and a place that allows us—gives us permission—to pause. To look inside and to embrace what is here, what is alive and well. To embrace our enoughness.

Think of this "sanctuary" space as a dose of grace.

It bestows gifts upon us... stillness, gladness, calm, mystery, delight, discovery, learning and peace. This resonates because it is in our DNA to be renewed, nourished, replenished and spiritually hydrated.

So, welcome to our journaling journey, as we uncover, embrace and savor. I'm so glad we are on this journey together.

Gratefully, life seems to ignore the script we have in our mind. And when that happens, we walk. We walk toward, or we walk away. Either way, we begin a journey—a pilgrimage to find or restore or give or heal or embrace; to forget or to bury or perhaps, just to have the deck of our world re-shuffled.

In writing we honor who we are and what is inside.

We give it a voice. Journaling is self-care. And self-care is our invitation to self-love, befriending our own heart.

Even with the cleansing, soul care is owning the gift of the "not easy to see" stuff.

We are, every single one of us, wounded. That is a gift.
We are, every single one of us, broken. And that is a gift.

We are blessedly human, and we do indeed walk one another home.

Befriending our woundedness is not a solo act. Yes, I know. It doesn't always feel that way. I look, but don't see any gift. Because I see brokenness and woundedness as impediments or disabilities, to be tidied up, overcome or prayed away. What I don't see is that in the invitation to befriend my "untidy" self, is the invitation to embrace the beauty and the wonder.

I will admit that there is comfort donning my cape, morphing into Mr. Tidy OCD, an emotional life fix-it hero. And I know why. It distracts and protects me, because there's a part of me that is afraid to pause, to befriend my scattered and wounded self. To let myself be loved for being this wonderfully messy imperfect me.

Grace, it turns out, is WD40 for the soul.

There are significant issues in our world (in my world) that invite and require investment and healing; and I want to show up. And I want to bring my real self, my whole self, and spill light in any small way that I can. But today reminded me that I cannot forget, in my fixation to "make sense" of everything... along the way (even the messy way)... I don't want to miss the small gifts of life, the serendipitous gifts of grace, the presence of the holy, and the gentle dose of the sacred reflected in our everyday, and extraordinarily ordinary world.

Ways to Use this Journal

I've been asked, too often in my life, what I believe. Here's the odd part; I have never once been asked about what nourishes my soul. Or to list what moves me. Or for stories about what warms my blood, sends gooseflesh up my arms, makes me want to dance, make me love life, or laugh and cry at the same time. I've been asked about what is appropriate, but never about what is important. This journal seeks to ask these important questions. I've always been tempted by, enamored with, smitten with arrival. Like the four year old child, five minutes out of the driveway on any family trip, "Are we there yet?" The notion that we arrive somewhere is never good for our blood pressure.

This journal doesn't require you to follow the page numbers. There is no chronological requirement or necessity. Find the pages that resonate, and start there. Go with themes that invite, return to themes for seconds.

I encourage you to set aside time every day (even if only 15 minutes) and know that catharsis is a good thing. Don't be afraid to write without editing. Here's the good news: Journaling is not a test or contest or beauty pageant. There is no need to impress. When I journal, I can discard the question, "Am I doing it right"?

Don't be afraid to use crayon in addition to pen and ink. Feel free to doodle or draw or paint. Tape photos to the page to remind you of what fills you with joy, with wonder, with sadness, with longing

Let this journal be your invitation to embrace serendipitous gifts of grace.

—*Terry Hershey*

glad to be alive

Someone asked me, "So. What's this journal for anyway?" My answer, "It's about the invitation and permission to re-train our eyes and mind. To see the sacred in the ordinary."

. . .

This spiritual practice opens our eyes to the gifts—the abundant simple pleasures— that surround us.

. . .

Write about a simple pleasure that happened, that you enjoyed, in the past day.

sacred place

We do not go there
merely to fulfill an
obligation.
We do not go there just
to be a good person.
We do not go there to
impress people we know.
We go there because if
we don't go, we lose a
part of our soul.

. . .

*Where are your sacred
places?*

sanctuary

Finish this sentence: I need
sanctuary because...

. . .

*Where is your sanctuary? What
are the ingredients that make it
sanctuary for you. (If you wish,
draw / color or paste a photo)*

sufficiency

With grace, we live from sufficiency. We affirm others, share credit, encourage and compliment friends, family, co-workers, we receive compliments gladly, we stop beating ourselves up.

How do you know when you're making choices from a place of sufficiency?

delight

I learned that the opposite of depression is not happiness, but delight. Grace fuels delight. Grace tumbles into our lives, and we are spontaneously surprised by the goodness and beauty of living.

What inspires you—keeps the fire going inside or keeps you from being stuck?

journey

Take a walk. The distance doesn't have to be far nor the walk strenuous. Choose a destination (two to five minutes away) — around the block, to the end of the street, through a park, around your garden. I want you to walk to that destination as quickly as possible, thinking only about the destination, as if you had on blinders. When you arrive, pause. Literally. For at least two or three minutes. Breathe. Now, return using the exact same route, only this time I want you to take at least twenty minutes. You can dawdle, meander or mosey, your choice.

. . .

What do you see that you missed the first time? What do you hear or smell or notice?

. . .

Everything that is newly noticed is an epiphany, an invitation to amazement.

resilience

Resilience is what happens when we give up control and are willing to embrace the ambiguity. And in that ambiguity, to hear the wing beats of butterflies.

. . .

Tell me what hearing the wing beats of butterflies makes you think of. What comes to mind, and stirs in your heart and spirit?

vulnerability

The culture we live in tells
us that strength is primarily
power and control. What would
it mean if power is found in
vulnerability?

. . .

*In what ways is vulnerability—
tenderness, humility—power?
What does it mean to be strong
on the inside?*

ambiguity

*What does it mean to
"invite all of life in"?
What does it mean
to welcome the parts
that don't make
sense? To not rush
to fix ambiguity?*

live
slow

To live *slow*
instead of fast?
To *be* instead of do?
To embrace *renewal*
instead of exhaustion?
To practice *presence*
instead of distraction?

. . .

*What does life look like if
we practice the first and
not the second?*

. . .

*What does life look like if
we practice the second
and not the first?*

replenishment

Think of times of quenching hunger
or thirst, water after a long walk or
work in the garden.

. . .

What are the "practices"—the places /
people / experiences—that allow you
to slow down, to be replenished and
to be present? Which might you
access this week?

subtraction

Is it possible that we change
the way we live, not by
addition, but by subtraction?
Make a list of things (including
mental script, stuff to which
we cling, unhealthy practices)
in your life that you could let go
of, "subtract," to allow for more
authenticity and balance.

empty space

Think about your life and
the amount of empty
space or empty time
you see there.

. . .

*Does the empty space
require an "activity"?*

diversions

"By means of a diversion, a man can avoid his own company twenty-four hours a day."

—Blaise Pascal

What are ways you avoid your own company? What in our culture makes diversions so addictive?

pay attention

For one day (OK, 30 minutes!)
this week, turn off your mobile
devices. Put away the lists
or work or pile of papers that
beckon. Sit still. Pay attention.
Let your words spill.

overwhelmed

When and where do you
feel overwhelmed?

. . .

Finish this sentence:
Sometimes I *choose*
to live overwhelmed
because...

obstacles

Which of these obstacles get in your way? Stress, distraction, hurry, if only, perfection syndrome, victim, anger, hate, playing the right notes? All of the above?

nourish

Our soul cannot thrive without nutrients.
It becomes anemic or withered or weak.
We experience a loss of creativity, joy,
presence, listening, vibrancy. And an
absence of peace.

*What or who is feeding that part
of your soul that nurtures peace
and well-being?*

. . .

*Where is that place that
doesn't require performance or
manipulation or retribution?*

self care

What is often the case (I'm
speaking personally) is that
I don't see the sacred in me
during times of pain or duress
or untidiness. Our invitation
here is self-care.

. . .

*If you could make time and
space to replenish, what would
that look like?*

. . .

*What allows you to slow down,
to stop for self-care?*

be yourself

Are there parts of you that have been put on hold, or withheld, or incessantly apologized about? Parts of you that are true and authentic, but someone or something told you to hide them or pretend they weren't there?

intention

Living intentionally
and fully alive—from a
place of groundedness
and internal peace—is
not a technique. There
is no list. But if we
demand one, chances
are, we pass life by—the
exquisite, the messy, the
enchanting, wondrous
delightful, untidy—on our
way to some place we
think we ought to be.

tidiness

What are the messages
we receive that tell
us our life cannot be
embraced or savored
until it is tidy or
manageable or
what's expected?

Where did (or do)
those messages
come from in
your life?

mindfulness

"There are two ways to wash dishes. The first is to wash the dishes in order to have clean dishes and the second is to wash the dishes in order to wash the dishes." —Thich Nhat Hahn

How does this resonate with you? What is the difference he is talking about? Write about an area of your life where this might apply.

remember

It's memory time. Think back
to childhood. What do you
remember savoring? Something
you saw, or tasted, or heard,
or smelled, or touched. An
experience when it felt like time
stopped. And when you recall it,
you smile, real big. We are told
that specific smells or sounds
instantly recreate memories.

play

Can you tell me the last time you were invited— given the permission— to be vulnerable, curious, lighthearted, inquisitive, spontaneous, intuitive and playful? To be filled with wonderment and laughter? How did you respond? If I invited you today, what would you say?

dance with your heart

Have you ever danced
with your heart?
What comes alive there?
What wakes up?
What is invited?

awareness

Tell me about your day.
What did you notice?
What did you hear?
What did you admire?
What astonished you?
What would you like to see again?
What was most tender?
What was most wonderful?
What did you think
was happening?

the present moment

Write about the times
(moments, encounters,
happenstances) when you
were glad to be alive in
your own skin. And don't
try to analyze it...
just sayin'.

just be

A man sat on his front porch smoking his pipe and rocking in his chair. A group of younger people walked by and asked, "So what are you doing old man?" He paused for a spell, and then said, "How soon do you need to know?"

Where are the places you can be / go that are not tied to performance or "productivity"?

enough

*What happens when
we can embrace,
"I am enough"?*

*What does it
mean to live
"from acceptance"
rather than "for
acceptance"?*

open your senses

Spend some more time this week sitting on a garden bench or a chair or a blanket on the grass. Give yourself permission to sit a spell.

. . .

What do you see, hear, taste, touch or smell? Name them. When we name the senses, we are grounded.

. . .

Now close your eyes, and say (to yourself or aloud), "It is enough."

gratitude

Gratitude allows us to be grounded. Connected with our senses. Gratitude and being present does our heart good.

. . .

Make a list... Today I am grateful for... (Notice that when we name a gratitude, we don't add the words *but* or *if* or *when...*)

stillness

When we stop the
noise, we make
space to practice
the sacrament of the
present. I am here. To
see. To listen. To touch.
To give. To heal.

Where do you
give back?
In what choices,
places, and
connections
do you find
meaning?

pause

Try any of these: buy
a flower, pick a flower,
savor a cup of coffee,
watch people, sit on
a park bench, count
clouds, look into a
baby's face, watch
birds at a feeder, visit a
beach, close your eyes
while on the commuter
train or bus, *fill in the
blank...*

. . .

*What happens, inside,
when you pause? Sit
with that moment
as long as you want.
Write about what you
experienced.*

wonder

Describe a time when you had gooseflesh. Describe what were you feeling in those moments. Here are some possibilities: glad to be alive, light-hearted, joyful, connected, alive in the moment.

What gets in the way or discourages moments of gooseflesh? What places, experiences, or people in your life encourage or invite moments of gooseflesh?

grace

When we live in a world
without grace, we live
small.
What does it mean to
you to live small?
. . .
How might you relate
to any of these?
- *Apologize for
  emotions,*
- *discount any
  compliment,*
- *spend energy needing
  to please or impress,*
- *feel like a victim,*
- *believe that
  courage or hope or
  fearlessness belong
  to someone else*

sufficiency

If we do not bring it with us,
we will not find it here. What is
it that we "bring" with us that
enables us to live in gratitude,
trust, respect, wholeness, and
responsibility?

replenishment

We often have places
and practices and people
in our life that nourish
us, but they are easily
unnoticed. Let's take
time to notice them.
Name them here.

interruptions

We tell ourselves that we could
learn to pause and practice
awareness once we "take care
of" all the interruptions.
What happens if instead you
focus on seeing, embracing,
savoring the interruptions?

spiritual hydration

When I pause, I trigger those parts of my soul...*the space to savor, relish, value, honor, share, welcome, invite, see, touch, celebrate, wonder, feel, to experience grace*...where renewal can be born.

Let's practice using one of those verbs–*savor or relish or celebrate for example*–in writing or sketching what I am seeing... that this moment is real. And good for my soul...)

the present moment

Make a "freedom to loll" date. A Sabbath date. (Here's part of my list... Meal with a friend / walking my dog / watching a butterfly cabaret / listening to music that soothes my spirit / meandering / playing with a child or watching children play / reading a book / counting clouds / sitting in the park people watching...)

. . .

What's on your "freedom to loll" list?

stillness

Describe a time / place
where you were able to just
be without evaluating or
measuring the experience.
Draw a picture or tell a
story about that time /
place / experience.

enough

After an ordinary
moment (a sip of coffee
or tea, the light slanting
through the window,
a hug, a cerulean blue
sky, a smile from a
friend, laughter...) say
to yourself (or out loud),
It is enough.

. . .

*What messages do you
get that tell you this
moment is not enough?*

. . .

*Where do the messages
come from and why do
we listen?*

gratitude

In pausing we see. In seeing we "weigh" things differently. When we weigh things differently, we practice gratitude.

Make a list of the things, people, and experiences in your life that you weigh as important or essential or vital. Take a moment and use your list as a gratitude prayer.

stillness

What are the gifts of stillness? What messages have you been given (or given yourself) about stillness? Why is it so tempting to need to justify or validate moments / times of stillness?

pause

We all have two spaces:
one for achievement
and accomplishment
and productivity and
busyness. The other
is for stillness and
pausing and music and
silence and waiting and
unrepentant napping.

. . .

*Where does your
spirit feel safe? What
happens to your mind
and heart there?*

. . .

*Where do you feel most
unhurried and settled?*

grace

Ordinary moments are the hiding place of the holy. Grace, presence, beauty and wonder are discovered in ordinary moments and ordinary days and ordinary interruptions.

. . .

What does it mean to let yourself be embraced by grace? When has that happened to you?

blessings

Let's talk about everyday blessings. What is on your list? We know (but easily forget) that these elements of the ordinary nourish, heal, and sustain. They offer hope, a will to live, wonder, fortitude, and a generosity of spirit.

ABOUT THE AUTHOR

Terry Hershey is an author, humorist, inspirational speaker, dad, ordained minister, golf addict, and smitten by French wine. He is the author of *This is the Life, Sanctuary, The Power of Pause* and *Soul Gardening*. He divides his time between designing sanctuary gardens and sharing his practice of mindfulness and savoring this life. Most days, you can find Terry out in his garden—on Vashon Island in the Puget Sound—because he believes that there is something fundamentally spiritual about dirt under your fingernails.

Cover and book design by Mark Sullivan

Copyright ©2020, Terry Hershey. All rights reserved.
ISBN 978-1-63253-373-9

Published by Franciscan Media
28 W. Liberty St.
Cincinnati, OH 45202
www.FranciscanMedia.org

Printed in the United States of America.
Printed on acid-free paper.
20 21 22 23 24 25 5 4 3 2 1